THE GARDNER MUSEUM HEIST

BY MICHAEL REGAN

CONTENT CONSULTANT
JENNIFER KREDER
PROFESSOR OF LAW
NORTHERN KENTUCKY UNIVERSITY

AMERICAN CRIME STORIES

Essential Library
An Imprint of Abdo Publishing | abdobooks.com

ABDOBOOKS.COM

Published by Abdo Publishing, a division of ABDO, PO Box 398166, Minneapolis, Minnesota 55439.

Printed in the United States of America, North Mankato, Minnesota.
092019
012020

THIS BOOK CONTAINS RECYCLED MATERIALS

Cover Photos: Art Collection 4/Alamy, top; incamerastock/Alamy, bottom; Shutterstock Images, frames
Interior Photos: Tom Herde/The Boston Globe/Getty Images, 4–5, 15, 29; iStockphoto, 6; Paul Marotta/Getty Images Entertainment/Getty Images, 9; Tom Landers/The Boston Globe/Getty Images, 12; Art Collection 4/Alamy, 16; ART Collection/Alamy, 19; Barney Burstein/Corbis/VCG/Getty Images, 20; Pictures Now/Alamy, 22; Red Line Editorial, 25; incamerastock/Alamy, 26; Gil Friedberg/The Boston Globe/Getty Images, 31; David L Ryan/The Boston Globe/Getty Images, 34–35; Everett Collection/Newscom, 38–39; Zuma Press, Inc./Alamy, 42; Joe Dennehy/The Boston Globe/Getty Images, 44; GL Archive/Alamy, 50–51; Lisa Bul/AP Images, 53; George Rizer/The Boston Globe/Getty Images, 54–55; Josh Reynolds/AP Images, 57; AP Images, 63; Jean-Christian Bourcart/Contour/Getty Images, 65; Steven Senne/AP Images, 70; John Tlumacki/The Boston Globe/Getty Images, 72–73; Photographee.eu/Shutterstock Images, 76; Gorgev/Shutterstock Images, 80; Richard Nowitz/National Geographic Image Collection/Alamy, 83; sanjeri/iStockphoto, 86; Stillman Rogers/Alamy, 90–91; Suzanne Kreiter/The Boston Globe/Getty Images, 96

Editor: Charly Haley
Series Designer: Melissa Martin

LIBRARY OF CONGRESS CONTROL NUMBER: 2019941939

PUBLISHER'S CATALOGING-IN-PUBLICATION DATA

Names: Regan, Michael, author.
Title: The Gardner Museum heist / by Michael Regan
Description: Minneapolis, Minnesota: Abdo Publishing, 2020 | Series: American crime stories | Includes online resources and index.
Identifiers: ISBN 9781532190094 (lib. bdg) | ISBN 9781532175947 (ebook)
Subjects: LCSH: Isabella Stewart Gardner Museum--Juvenile literature. | Robbery--Juvenile literature. | Art thefts--Juvenile literature. | Boston, Massachusetts--Juvenile literature. | Cold cases (Criminal investigation)--Juvenile literature.
Classification: DDC 364.16287--dc23

CONTENTS

CHAPTER ONE

THE BIGGEST ART THEFT

In the early morning hours after Saint Patrick's Day 1990, several students who had just left a party walked by the Isabella Stewart Gardner Museum in Boston, Massachusetts. They noticed a small unmarked car with what looked like two policemen sitting in the front seats. The students did not want to get arrested for underage drinking, so they kept walking.

However, it later became clear that those men were not police officers. The biggest art heist in world history happened at the Gardner Museum that night. Two thieves posed as policemen to gain access to the museum. Thirteen works of art—worth more than half a billion dollars together—were stolen. The heist revealed major flaws in the museum's security, including an unheeded warning from

The Isabella Stewart Gardner Museum in March 1990

ISABELLA
STEWART
GARDNER
MUSEUM

an FBI agent about the possibility of a robbery years before the heist occurred.

There are many theories about who planned and committed the heist, with a list of suspects ranging from petty thieves to experienced mobsters to even a fake California screenwriter. The most likely perpetrators appear to be in some way related to organized crime in Boston. As of mid-2019, the crime had still not been solved.

The Heist

The heist began at 1:24 a.m. on March 18, 1990.[1] Two men, dressed as policemen, pushed the buzzer at the door of the museum. One of the museum's night security guards, Richard Abath, demanded to know what they wanted. The fake policemen said they were responding to a call about some sort

The Gardner Museum, which opened in 1903, is located in Boston's Fenway neighborhood.

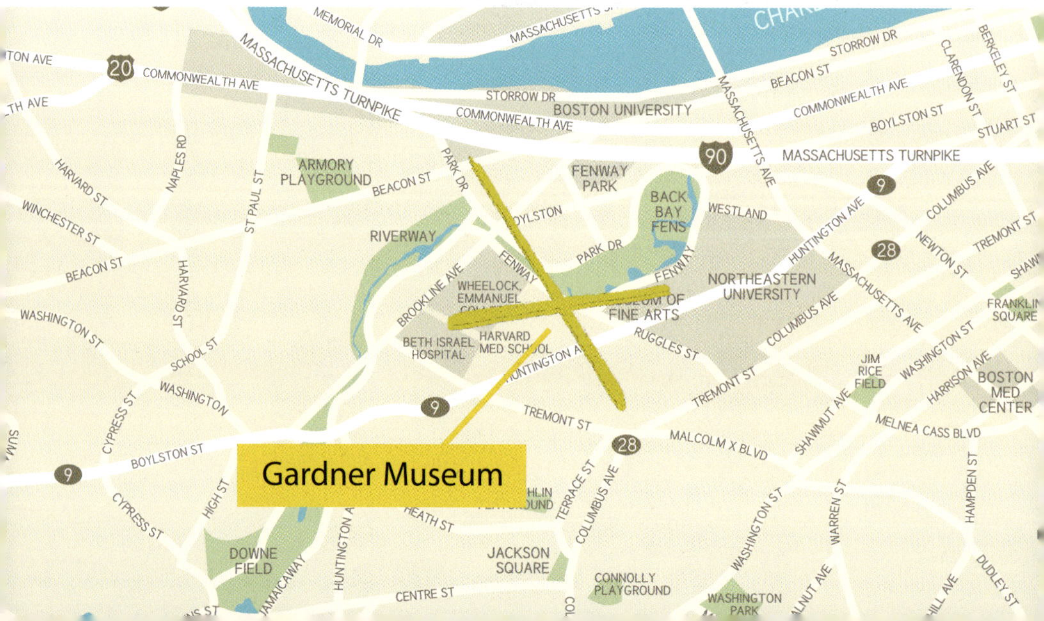

FAMOUS ART HEISTS

The Gardner Museum heist in 1990 is one of many famous art thefts in history. In 1911, Leonardo da Vinci's *Mona Lisa* was stolen from its easel in France's Louvre museum. Several years later, an Italian man who used to work at the Louvre confessed he had the painting. He was sentenced to six months in jail for the theft.

In 2003, three paintings worth about $8 million were stolen from the Whitworth Art Gallery in Manchester, United Kingdom. Police later got a tip that the artwork had been left in a public bathroom. Police found the paintings there, stuffed into a cardboard tube. There was also a note explaining that the robbery had been committed to show how poor the security was at the gallery.

In 2017, a 220-pound (100 kg) gold coin was stolen from the Bode Museum in Berlin, Germany. The thieves used a wheelbarrow to haul the coin away. The coin was worth about $4.5 million. The thieves were later arrested.

of disturbance at the museum. The claim seemed reasonable to Abath because it was Saint Patrick's Day, and there were a lot of parties going on in the area. The guard let them in through the museum employees' entrance. This action was in violation of the museum's security protocol. The thieves were now inside the museum.

Once inside, one of the phony policemen said Abath looked like a person who had an outstanding warrant for arrest. He demanded to see Abath's ID. Then the thieves handcuffed Abath. The second security guard arrived. He also was handcuffed. When the men asked why they were being arrested, the policemen said it was not an arrest but a robbery. They told the two guards to not make any trouble.

The second guard said, "Don't worry. They don't pay me enough to get hurt."[2] The thieves used duct tape and handcuffs to incapacitate the guards in the museum basement. Before heading back upstairs, the robbers took the guards' wallets. They said, "We know where you live. Do as I say and no harm will come to you."[3] The thieves also told them not to tell the police about the robbery and that they'd be rewarded for their silence.

Dutch Room

Leaving the guards in the basement, the thieves started going through the museum's art exhibits. In the Dutch Room, they found three paintings by the famous Rembrandt van Rijn, usually referred to as simply Rembrandt. His work called *Christ in the Storm on the Sea of Galilee* was remarkably large, at 63 inches (160 cm) tall and 50 inches (127 cm) wide. It was too heavy for the thieves to carry, so they threw the framed painting on the floor. Through the broken glass, they cut the art piece from its wooden frame.

The thieves also stole Rembrandt's *A Lady and Gentleman in Black*. It was almost 52 inches (132 cm) tall and 43 inches (109 cm)

Each year, more than 50,000 pieces of art are stolen worldwide.[4]

wide. The painting was also cut from its frame so it would fit in the getaway car.

A third large Rembrandt painting, a self-portrait, was almost stolen as well. However, the portrait was painted on a wood panel, and the thieves must have decided it was too difficult to carry, so they left it behind after taking it down from the wall. Instead, they took Rembrandt's smaller self-portrait etching, which was the size of a postage stamp.

The Dutch Room also held what was by far the most rare and valuable piece of all the artwork stolen during the heist. It was the small painting called *The Concert* by Johannes Vermeer.[5] Still in the Dutch Room, the robbers also took an oil painting on wood, *Landscape with an Obelisk* by Govaert Flinck.

The Gardner Museum has more than two dozen galleries and rooms, including a courtyard.

Before leaving the Dutch Room, the thieves took one more object. It was a bronze Chinese cup called a *gu* that stood 10 inches (25 cm) tall. It was among the oldest objects in the museum's collection.

The Short Gallery

In the museum's Short Gallery, the thieves focused on a flag from French leader Napoleon's regimental guards. The banner itself was in a glass case that the robbers couldn't remove from the wall. So they just took the finial (an ornamental eagle) that sat atop the flagpole.

The first recorded major art heist was in 1473. Polish pirates stole a Dutch triptych, a three-panel hinged painting, from a church altar. It is now in a museum in Gdańsk, Poland.[7]

The robbers also turned their attention to two glass frames in the Short Gallery. Smashing the glass, they took five works by Edgar Degas. Together, those five were valued at about $100,000 at the time of the heist.[6]

The Blue Room

The last painting missing after the heist was Édouard Manet's *Chez Tortoni*. It was stolen from the Blue Room on the first floor of the museum. Although the painting went missing on the night of the heist, authorities say it is not clear whether the fake policemen were the ones who took it.

BLUE ROOM STRANGENESS

The Manet painting taken the night of the heist was in the Blue Room. The room's electronic sensors did not detect entry into the room, even though they had earlier detected the security guard doing his nightly rounds. Could the sensors have been turned off for a while? The robbers could have done this. They knew where the museum's security center was located and removed the security tape recordings that showed their movements in the museum.

The museum hired a security consultant, Steven Keller, to review the theft. He concluded that the infrared movement detector had been working all the time on the night of the robbery. Keller personally tried and failed to gain access to the Blue Room without being detected. He concluded that someone other than the people who had stolen the rest of the art had taken the painting from the Blue Room. Who that someone was is still a mystery.

Before the thieves left, one of them returned to the basement. One of the guards said later that he could hear the robber breathing as he stood near him. The guard must have worried what the criminal might do to him because he had witnessed the crime. But without a word, the robber left the basement. In the 81 minutes between the time they entered the museum and when they left, the thieves made two trips to their vehicle carrying the stolen art. Then they departed, taking some security videotapes with them.

Robbery Revealed

No one other than the thieves and the handcuffed guards knew the robbery had occurred until early the next morning when two daytime security guards arrived. The guards rang the security buzzer to be let into the building. There was no response. They thought the night guards might be sleeping, so they started tapping on windows in hopes of waking them. Getting no response, they called their supervisor. Within ten minutes, the supervisor arrived and unlocked the door. The inside of the museum was silent.

Reporters gathered as Gardner Museum officials announced the heist to the public.

GLOBAL ART THEFT

The Federal Bureau of Investigation (FBI) estimates that art theft worth billions of dollars is committed globally each year. Italy and France have the highest amount of art theft, according to the International Criminal Police Organization (INTERPOL). Other countries, such as Afghanistan, Iraq, and Syria, have had valuable historical sites and objects looted during times of war.

Countries around the world take differing approaches to dealing with art crime. In Italy, 300 police officers are assigned to art crime.[8] Greece's constitution provides for protecting its cultural heritage. The United States has a small FBI Art Crime Team, and the United Kingdom's Scotland Yard hires archaeologists to track down stolen art. Former FBI special agent Robert Wittman says, "[Art crime] is rated the fourth largest criminal activity in the world, behind drugs, guns and money laundering."[9]

The guard supervisor called the museum's head of security, Lyle Grindle, who told him to call the police. Soon, police officers spread out through the building, not knowing whether the thieves were still inside. With flashlights glaring and guns drawn, the police entered the Dutch Room. There, they saw broken glass and picture frames—the first indications of the heist. Meanwhile, in the basement, police were relieved to find the two night guards bound but still alive. The full weight of what had been stolen was not evident until later in the day, when the museum director and curator surveyed the losses.

CHAPTER TWO

THE STOLEN ART

A total of 13 pieces were stolen during the Gardner Museum heist. Eleven of the artworks were paintings or sketches. The final two were ten-inch (25 cm) tall bronze works.[1]

Christ in the Storm on the Sea of Galilee

Gardner purchased *Christ in the Storm on the Sea of Galilee* for $29,100 in 1898.[2] It was the most valuable of the Rembrandt paintings taken during the heist. It was painted in 1633 when Rembrandt was 27 years old. This piece was an illustration of the New Testament Bible passage about Christ and his disciples on a stormy sea. The artwork was the only seascape known to have been painted by the artist, which added to its value.

Gardner Museum officials presented images of the stolen artworks to the media and the public after the heist to explain what was stolen.

Christ in the Storm on the Sea of Galilee

The Dutch painter Rembrandt van Rijn was born in 1606 and died in 1669. Rembrandt painted during what was known as the Baroque art period. Later art critics viewed the Baroque style as odd, exaggerated, and even grotesque. Rembrandt's works were different in that his artwork was known for realistically capturing his subjects. Art critic Lloyd Schwartz described *Christ in the Storm on the Sea of Galilee* as one of Rembrandt's "most dramatic and dynamic images."[3] Even its size was impressive. It was approximately five feet (1.5 m) high and four feet (1.2 m) wide.

Two More Rembrandts

Rembrandt's work titled *A Lady and Gentleman in Black* was painted in 1633. It depicted a well-dressed husband and wife. Rembrandt was 26 or 27 years old when he painted it. This was one of his works that brought him early fame. The painting was purchased by Gardner for $63,000 in 1898.[4]

A Lady and Gentleman in Black is thought to be the artist's first painting showing a married couple together. He usually painted each person in separate portraits called pendants. The colors in the painting were mostly rich and dark. However, he also included intricately detailed white lace collars on both the subjects. This painting was also quite large. It was more than four feet (1.2 m) tall and 3.5 feet (1.1 m) wide.

The thieves also stole a small self-portrait created by Rembrandt in 1633. The etching, titled *Portrait of the Artist as a Young Man*, was only two inches (5 cm) by 1.75 inches (4.45 cm). It was purchased by Gardner for approximately $120.[5] When the self-portrait was completed, Rembrandt was already a famous and successful artist.

Landscape with an Obelisk

Painted in 1638, *Landscape with an Obelisk* was mistakenly thought to be a Rembrandt original until shortly before the museum heist. Gardner purchased the painting in 1900 for almost $22,000.[6] The work was actually painted by one of Rembrandt's students, Govaert Flinck, a Dutch artist who lived from 1615 to 1660.

CURRENT VALUE

Isabella Gardner bought the artwork that would be stolen in the 1990 museum heist back in the late 1800s and early 1900s. She paid almost $142,000 (equivalent to several million dollars in today's money) for the stolen artwork. Today, those 13 items could be worth between $600 million and $1 billion, according to Kathryn Graddy, dean of the International Business School at Brandeis University. Her expertise is the study of the value of auctioned art.

The tremendous value depends, of course, on the condition of the art when it is found or returned. Pieces that are well cared for would bring higher values. Another factor in these pieces' value is that they were part of the Gardner Museum heist. According to Graddy, "The fact that they've been stolen is going to give them more notoriety and value and not in a bad sense."[7]

A Lady and Gentleman in Black

Landscape with an Obelisk

The landscape measured 21 inches (53 cm) high by 28 inches (71 cm) wide. Colors in the painting were mostly browns and grays. The scene depicted a cloudy day with a giant gnarled tree on one side and an obelisk on the other. An obelisk is a square pillar with a pyramid-shaped top.

The Ancient Chinese Gu and the Bronze Finial

The stolen Shang dynasty drinking cup, called a gu, dated back to about 1200 BCE. Gardner purchased the gu in 1922 for about $17,500.[8] With its intricately formed stem and base, it was characterized as one of the most elegant pieces in the Gardner collection.

Created in 1813 or 1814, the finial that topped a regimental flag was bought by Gardner for $300 in 1880.[9] The flag remained in the Gardner Museum because the robbers could not get it out of its case. Similar finials could be purchased today for a much lower price.

The Concert

Johannes Vermeer lived his whole life in Delft, the Netherlands. He was born in 1632 and died in 1675. He began his career painting biblical themes, but his most popular works came later. These masterpieces were of daily life inside of homes. Fewer than 40 of Vermeer's paintings still exist.

Vermeer painted *The Concert* sometime between 1663 and 1666. Gardner bought the painting at an auction for about $5,600 in 1892.[10]

Vermeer died without fame or money. His work *The Concert* remained essentially unknown for 100 years.

The Concert is considered the most valuable piece stolen during the Gardner Museum heist.

MEMORIES

In early 1990, artist Sophie Calle was exhibiting some of her works at Boston's Institute of Contemporary Art. While in Boston, she often visited the Gardner Museum and particularly liked Vermeer's *The Concert*. Shortly after her visits, *The Concert* was stolen during the Gardner Museum heist. Because she remembered *The Concert* so fondly, she wanted to honor the stolen work.

Calle went to the museum and asked its staff members what they remembered about the stolen artwork and how the pieces had affected them. She then consolidated the thoughts, framed them, and paired the responses with pictures of the empty spaces where the stolen artworks had hung on the walls of the museum. The purpose of her exhibit was to change the perception of the heist from loss and sorrow to one of creativity and life. The series of pictures was titled *Last Seen . . .*

It was the first major work of art she purchased. *The Concert* was valued at $300 million in 2017.[11] It was the most expensive work of art taken in the heist. *The Concert*'s high value is due to its rarity. Vermeer made only a relatively small number of paintings. Almost 100 years after being bought by Isabella Gardner, the value of *The Concert* had increased exponentially.

Works by Degas

Edgar Degas was a French painter and sculptor who lived from 1834 to 1917. He was connected to an artistic movement called Impressionism. In this art form, the concern was for the feeling or impression of the moment, rather than strict adherence to details. Degas socialized with other now-famous artists, including Claude Monet, Édouard Manet, and Pierre-Auguste Renoir. Degas was famous for his ordinary life subjects that included dancers, jockeys, and race horses.

Five works by Degas were stolen from the Gardner Museum. Two were charcoal sketches done in 1884. The sketches, which were twelve inches (30 cm) by eight inches (20 cm), were of dancers and musical instruments. Gardner purchased them in 1919 for a total of $90.[12]

The other three, two sketches and a watercolor painting, were created between 1857 and 1888. The subjects were jockeys and horses. The three items cost Gardner about $750 in 1919.[13]

Chez Tortoni

Manet's *Chez Tortoni* was a painting of a young man sitting in a café, wearing a top hat, with a wine glass next to him. Édouard Manet was born in Paris, France, in 1832 and died there in 1883. Many of his paintings were from drawings of ordinary people he created while socializing in the cafés in Paris. Manet painted *Chez Tortoni* in approximately 1875. Gardner purchased it years later, in 1922, for $3,400.[14]

While *Chez Tortoni* went missing on the night of the Gardner Museum heist, it was the only item that investigators thought might have been taken separately from the other works of

THE 13 STOLEN ARTWORKS

ARTWORK	ARTIST	YEAR BOUGHT BY GARDNER
Bronze eagle finial	---	1880
Portrait of the Artist as a Young Man	Rembrandt	1886
The Concert	Johannes Vermeer	1892
Christ in the Storm on the Sea of Galilee	Rembrandt	1898
A Lady and Gentleman in Black	Rembrandt	1898
Landscape with an Obelisk	Govaert Flinck	1900
Cortège aux environs de Florence	Edgar Degas	1919
La Sortie de Pesage	Edgar Degas	1919
Study for the Programme de la Soirée Artistique du 15 Juin 1884 (Galerie Ponsin) (1 of 2)	Edgar Degas	1919
Study for the Programme de la Soirée Artistique du 15 Juin 1884 (Galerie Ponsin) (2 of 2)	Edgar Degas	1919
Three Mounted Jockeys	Edgar Degas	1919
Chez Tortoni	Édouard Manet	1922
Ancient Chinese gu	---	1922

Isabella Stewart Gardner began building up her art collection in the late 1800s. After opening her museum in 1903, she continued to add to the collection.

Chez Tortoni

art, due to the security measures of the Blue Room where the painting was located.

What Wasn't Taken

Isabella Stewart Gardner's art collection has more than 7,500 paintings, pieces of furniture, textiles, sculptures, silver items, and ceramics. Her first interest was in literary art, so she added 1,500 rare books to her museum. She also had an extensive assortment of archival objects. Those items are stored in a museum archive and may occasionally be displayed. The Gardner Museum reported that its 7,000 archived items come

REPAIRING THE DAMAGE

In 1985, Willem de Kooning's *Woman-Ochre* was stolen from the University of Arizona (UA) Museum of Art. Thirty-two years later, a New Mexico antiques dealer contacted the museum and said he had obtained the painting at an estate sale. The painting was worth $100 million. Like several of the Gardner Museum paintings, it was cut from its frame and rolled tightly so it could be more easily carried. Those actions can severely decrease the value of a painting, but repairs are possible.

In March 2019, UA museum staff chose the J. Paul Getty Museum and Getty Conservation Institute in Los Angeles, California, to restore *Woman-Ochre*. Plans for the restoration of the painting included reattaching the painting to the bits left behind when it was cut. Microscopic bits of paint would need to be stabilized, requiring research into the materials that were originally used. The restoration was expected to be complete by 2020, with a plan to display the restored painting at the Getty before returning it to the UA museum.[17]

"from ancient Rome, Medieval Europe, Renaissance Italy, Asia, the Islamic world and 19th-century France and America."[15]

Anthony Amore, the Gardner Museum's director of security in 2019, is puzzled by why the robbers chose the items they stole. "It just makes no sense to me," he says.[16] One painting left behind was the most valuable painting in Boston. Titian's *The Rape of Europa* was located on the third floor of the museum. The criminals did not even go up to that floor.

CHAPTER THREE

AN EARLY WARNING

As the investigation into the Gardner Museum heist continued, it became clear that this crime may have been preventable. An FBI agent had warned the museum's board of directors about security flaws nine years before the 13 valuable art pieces were stolen. But the board did not take action to better secure the museum.

The warning came from FBI Special Agent Edward Clark, who worked undercover in the early 1980s, acting as a buyer of stolen artwork. Clark's work resulted in the arrest of two Boston organized-crime figures. One of them was Louis Royce. Royce revealed that he was planning a robbery at the Gardner Museum while telling Clark about selling art from an unrelated robbery.

Two FBI agents investigate the crime scene on the morning of the Gardner Museum heist.

THE BEGINNING

The Gardner Museum was founded and funded by Isabella Stewart Gardner. She and her husband, Jack, married in 1860. Gardner began collecting rare books in 1878 and eventually moved on to collecting art. In 1891, she inherited $1.75 million when her father died. That amount was equivalent to nearly $50 million in 2019. Fueled by this inheritance, the Gardners expanded their art collection. In 1896, they decided that their home was too small for their growing collection. They had the idea to build a museum. Gardner collected more than 15,000 pieces of art throughout her lifetime.[2]

Shortly after her husband's death in 1898, Gardner bought the land where the museum would be built. In 1899, construction began on the museum. It was completed in 1901. Gardner moved into the fourth-story apartments in the new building that year. In 1902, she placed her sculptures, rare books, furniture, decorative arts, and paintings throughout the lower three floors. The grand opening of the museum was on January 1, 1903.

Shortly after Royce's arrest, nine years before the Gardner heist, two FBI agents held a meeting with the Gardner museum's director, assistant director, and security director. One of those agents was Clark. He opened with, "You've got a problem, my friends. Some people have found a hole in your security system."[1]

Clark went on to outline the possible heist scenarios he had learned about from interviewing Royce. The first was to create a smoke-bomb distraction during a regularly scheduled Tuesday night concert. These concerts took place in the Tapestry Room, the largest open space in the museum. During the smoky confusion, the thieves could run off with several works of art located on the first floor of the museum.

A second possible plan proved to be prophetic. The FBI agent said the robbers might dress up as policemen or women in distress and ask for entrance into the museum after it had closed for the night. He also said a security guard might provide information to the thieves about the museum's security system. Although alarmed by this warning from Special Agent Clark, the museum's director and security personnel were not able to convince the museum's board of trustees to pay for upgrading security.

Visitors admire artwork in the Gardner Museum's Short Gallery in 1966. The Gardner Museum was well-known long before the famous 1990 heist.

Royce and the Gardner Museum

Louis Royce spent most of his life in and out of jail for various crimes. He robbed banks and other establishments. He gained acceptance into Boston's organized crime society by robbing a courthouse evidence locker. The locker contained money and other incriminating evidence against a big-time bookmaker, or bookie—someone who runs the bets in an illegal gambling ring. Even though Royce was arrested and sent to jail, the bookie was released because all the evidence was gone. Royce had proved his trustworthiness to the mob.

Royce had run away from home in his early teen years and lived on the streets of Boston. One of the places he found to

ART OBJECT ID

The black market trade of art objects is one of the largest areas of international crime. To combat these crimes, the Object ID system helps identify art objects. The system was designed to be easily understood by both artwork professionals and law enforcement agencies. Museums, law enforcement agencies, art and antique appraisers, insurance agencies, and the art community collaborated on developing the system. It is an international standard that presents the information needed to quickly identify an art object. Each ID includes information such as the title of the piece, the subject, the materials used in its creation, and measurements. A book, *Introduction to Object ID: Guidelines for Making Records That Describe Art, Antiques, and Antiquities*, was published in 1999 to make the standards readily available to all interested parties. The book even details the best way to photograph the art.

sleep overnight was inside the Gardner Museum. He found he could enter the museum before closing time and hide under a desk on the third floor without being noticed. It was during this time that he realized the museum would be an easy target. Although Royce was tied to Clark's 1981 warning about a possible heist, the actual crime has not been pinned on him. He was serving a 12-year prison sentence at the time of the heist. However, the FBI considered Royce to be a suspect in the sense that agents believed he had information about who did commit the robbery.

Pleas Unheeded

Lyle Grindle was the security director of the Gardner Museum in 1981 when Clark and the FBI issued their warning. Grindle's job was to protect the valuable collection of art within the museum. He was also in charge of improvements to the building's security system. It was a challenging job. The museum's board of directors was hesitant to offer up money for any building upgrades, including security. Built in the early 1900s, the building had never had any major upgrades made to its plumbing, electrical, or ventilation systems.

After the FBI visit, Grindle vigorously tried to get the museum's security measures updated throughout the 1980s. He pleaded with the museum's board of directors, asking for

A visitor admires the Gardner Museum in 1984. Throughout the 1980s, museum staff members tried to obtain more money for security to protect the beloved art.

money for upgrades, but he was unsuccessful. They did not have the money, and there were no plans made to raise funds.

The board finally approved $1 million for museum projects in 1986—but few of the projects were security measures. There wasn't enough money to properly update security. The museum director in the mid-1980s, Rollin Hadley, told Grindle

that if he wanted more money, he'd have to raise it himself. So Grindle began writing letters to Boston area corporations asking for donations. He raised $50,000 and used the money to buy an alarm system that monitored for fire and broken windows. It was a start, but it still wasn't enough for a museum housing artwork worth billions of dollars.

In 1985, the board of directors did investigate whether the whole museum, including the security system, needed to be remodeled. An expert in fundraising campaigns, Caroline Standley, was hired to provide suggestions to the board. She proposed contacting wealthy Bostonians to contribute ongoing donations that would support the museum. However, the board members viewed fundraising efforts as equivalent to begging and thought they were above that. They dismissed the recommendation, and Standley resigned from her advisory position in 1987 out of frustration. She could not get the board members to approve any plan.

Gardner Staff Demoralized

The year after Standley resigned from her position with the Gardner Museum, the deputy director of the museum resigned, too. He said in a letter to a board member that he could not continue working "for the museum under the conditions of confusion, indecision, inadequate communication and a lack of defined and shared goals" from the board of directors.[3] More staff administrators were becoming frustrated with the board of directors as well. Within a year, museum director Hadley resigned, too, saying the board's refusal to set up a fundraising campaign had doomed him. Less than a year later, the Gardner Museum heist took place in the manner that the board had been warned about nine years earlier.

No Theft Insurance

In addition to apparently lacking in security measures, the Gardner Museum had no theft insurance at the time of the heist. The insurance premiums were deemed too high by the organization's board of directors. At the time, a spokesman for the museum said the collection was insured for damage but not theft. Insuring the collection at that time would have come to about $3 million a year. The total budget for the museum was only $2.8 million a year.[4] Underinsuring art collections was common at that time, according to a *New York Times* article. Museums and dealers usually carried some theft insurance but not for the full value of the total collection because of high insurance costs.

Empty frames are acting as placeholders for all the Gardner Museum heist pictures until they are returned. Isabella Gardner's will stated that nothing in the museum could be rearranged after her death.

Gardner's precisely worded will also played a part in the museum not being insured because she instructed that the museum could not buy new or substitute artwork. She wanted everything left just as it was at her death. So even if the museum did have insurance, it could not have used money gained from any insurance claims to replace stolen art.

ORGANIZED CRIME IN BOSTON

As of 2019, no one had ever been apprehended for stealing the Gardner Museum art. Several people have indicated they knew where the art was, but those leads never amounted to anything. As the case remains unsolved, there are still many theories about who did it.

According to Noah Charney, art history professor and editor of the book *Art Crime: Terrorists, Tomb Raiders, Forgers and Thieves*, "Art police say that most art crime since the 1960s has involved organized crime at

Like many American cities, Boston has a history of organized crime.

some point."[1] For the Gardner Museum heist, this would point to organized crime in Boston.

The Irish Gangs and the Italian Mafia

The earliest organized crime groups in the United States are said to be the Irish gangs. These gangs were well established by the late 1800s. The Irish gangs were very strong in the suburbs and cities around Boston during the mid-to-late 1900s. At the same time, the Italian Mafia controlled the north side of Boston. The first Cosa Nostra boss, Gaspare Messina, started the Boston family, a prominent Italian crime group, in 1916.

Over the years, power shifted between the Irish mob and the Italian Mafia, but at any given time, one of the two groups controlled crime in Boston. At the time of the Gardner Museum heist in 1990, the Italian and Irish groups were in control of nearly all criminal activity in the city. James "Whitey" Bulger was the boss of the Winter Hill Gang, part of the Irish mob. Leadership of the Italian Boston family had shifted to Raymond Patriarca Jr. There were few independent criminal operators.

There are a number of organized crime groups in the United States made up of people within the same ethnicity, with the same interests, or living in the same area.

Law enforcement agencies were actively investigating Boston's organized crime. In 1989, the FBI was able to record a meeting at which all leadership members of the Patriarca crime family were present. It was the first time the FBI had been able to listen to and record a Cosa Nostra induction ceremony. As a result, all of the leaders of the crime family were convicted of various crimes and sent to jail. These types of investigations meant law enforcement was familiar with Boston mobsters at the time of the Gardner Museum heist.

Bobby Donati

The FBI strongly suspected mobster Bobby Donati as one of the perpetrators of the Gardner Museum heist. The FBI had Donati under constant surveillance. The suspicions about Donati seemed to be supported by the work of former *Boston Globe* reporter and author Stephen Kurkjian. In April 2014, Kurkjian had sent a message to the convicted leader of the Italian Mafia, Vincent Ferrera. At the time, Ferrera was in prison. Kurkjian asked whether Ferrera would be willing to help solve the Gardner Museum heist. Ferrera never responded to Kurkjian in person. But in May 2014, Kurkjian received an anonymous phone call. The caller said he was an intermediary for Ferrera. During the conversation, the caller said that Donati had committed the heist. Donati had a motive for such a theft. He wanted to get his friend and mentor Ferrera out of jail.

Journalist Stephen Kurkjian speaks at an event in 2019. Working for the *Boston Globe*, Kurkjian was one of several reporters who investigated mob ties to the Gardner Museum heist.

According to the anonymous source, Donati had visited Ferrera in prison in 1990 and 1991 after the Mafia boss had been convicted of second-degree murder. During one of those visits, Donati told Ferrera that he would do something to get Ferrera out. Ferrera told Donati it was too risky, but he later heard about the Gardner heist. At their next prison visit, Donati reportedly admitted the robbery to Ferrera. Donati said he had buried the artwork, according to the anonymous caller. And his next task was to figure out a way to begin negotiating Ferrera's release. Before Donati could attempt those alleged negotiations, however, he was murdered as part of ongoing Mafia conflicts in September 1991. Although federal investigators were apparently aware of Donati, Kurkjian wrote in a 2018 news story that the FBI declined to publicly comment on Donati's potential involvement in the Gardner Museum heist. The crime has never officially been pinned on Donati.

Reissfelder and DiMuzio

Another theory points to other members of the Boston Mafia. In 2013, the FBI announced that after years of investigation, agents believed "with a high degree of confidence" that two local mobsters appeared to have carried out the heist.[2] Although federal agents did not publicly name the suspects or officially attribute the crime to anyone, journalists and others have said the 2013 FBI story suggested that the suspects were George Reissfelder and Leonard DiMuzio. Both suspects resembled sketches made by the police shortly after the heist.

Some organized crime art thefts are used to get art owners or their insurance companies to pay for the return of their artwork. This is known as artnapping.

George Reissfelder in 1982

Reissfelder and DiMuzio had regularly stopped at Carmello Merlino's repair shop. Merlino, who also had connections to the Mafia, reportedly bragged to two undercover informants that he had planned to get the artwork and turn it in for the reward. But before that could happen, he was arrested in connection with a different robbery in 1999 and went to jail, where he died in 2005. Merlino was offered leniency in his jail sentence if he would return the stolen artwork, but he could never produce the art. The people who believe Reissfelder and DiMuzio committed the heist theorize that they did it as part of Merlino's supposed plan. The two suspected thieves died shortly after the robbery, in 1991. Reissfelder died of a cocaine overdose. DiMuzio was found shot to death.

Guarente and Turner

If Reissfelder and DiMuzio did steal the artwork, investigators believe they probably gave it to mobster Bobby Guarente, who was a good friend of Donati. In addition to being a prominent Boston mob associate, Guarente was a convicted bank robber. Guarente influenced young criminal David Turner, who was still in high school when he met Guarente. Guarente taught Turner about Boston's criminal underworld. The FBI suspected that both Guarente and Turner had been involved in the Gardner Museum heist.

As one of several known Mafia associates, Turner was one of the FBI's early heist suspects. Investigators thought he matched the description of one of the robbers given by the security guards shortly after the heist. The FBI analyzed Turner's fingerprints at its crime lab but found no matches from the scene of the crime. When questioned by investigators, Turner said he didn't know anything about the stolen art. As of 2019, Turner was in prison for an unrelated crime, attempting to rob an armored-car headquarters in 1999. His prison sentence was set to last until 2025.

The FBI believed that Guarente received the stolen artwork from Turner, Reissfelder, and DiMuzio. Only two of these men would have theoretically stolen the art, because it's clear that only two men had dressed as police officers and entered the museum during the heist. But other people may have helped in unknown ways.

Under this theory, the FBI believed that Guarente held on to the stolen artwork until shortly after learning he had cancer in the early 2000s. At that point, agents theorize that Guarente gave at least some of the art to Robert Gentile, another close associate of Donati. This theory was based on a 2010 statement to the FBI from Guarente's wife, Elene. She spoke to investigators shortly after her husband's death. Bobby Guarente died in 2010 without ever revealing anything about the missing Gardner Museum artwork.

Robert Gentile

It was Elene Guarente's 2010 statement that first drew the FBI's attention to Gentile, despite Gentile's known, long-standing ties to the Mafia. Elene Guarente told the FBI that her husband had given Gentile two of the stolen paintings. Gentile denied the accusation. His crime associate's widow supposedly linked him to the missing artwork because he would not give her money.

Despite Gentile's denial, law enforcement officials still considered him a suspect. While searching Gentile's house after a 2012 drug bust, the FBI found police hats, badges, and a list of the stolen Gardner Museum art, along with possible black market prices. Additionally, an undercover FBI agent had secretly recorded Gentile offering him at least two of

ELENE GUARENTE

Elene Guarente was desperate for money after her husband Bobby's death. This eventually prompted her to go to the FBI with information about Gentile. The Italian restaurant she had opened had failed, and she was living on Social Security Disability payments. She told the FBI that her late husband had said Robert Gentile would provide for her by using the stolen Gardner Museum art. But when she asked Gentile to help her financially, he had refused, she said. Then she saw an FBI highway billboard advertising a $5 million reward for the Gardner paintings. She contacted the FBI and the security director of the museum to offer information. In return, she received $1,000 to fix the radiator of her car.

the paintings for $500,000 each. The date of that recording was not made public, but according to a Reuters news report, the fact that it happened was confirmed years later by a prosecutor during a court hearing for Gentile for an unrelated crime. One of Gentile's lawyers said that Gentile's recorded claim about having access to the stolen art was false; it was an attempt to scam people into giving him money. But Gentile didn't help his claims of innocence when he later failed a lie detector test with questions regarding the Gardner Museum heist. He was again recorded in a 2014 FBI sting operation, saying he could get the paintings—for the right price. Gentile never produced the art, and the sting operation ended when he was sent back to prison for a gun violation. Gentile might be one of the last two living people, along with Turner, with knowledge of the biggest art robbery in history. But like Turner, Gentile has not admitted anything to authorities.

Whitey Bulger

The FBI is not the only law enforcement agency that suspected the Boston mob was connected to the Gardner Museum heist. "The paintings are in the West of Ireland," according to former Scotland Yard investigator Charles Hill.[3] Scotland Yard is a large law enforcement agency in London, England. Hill was a part of its Art and Antiques Unit for 20 years. Upon retiring, he became a private investigator specializing in art theft and was involved in the recovery of stolen art in several high-profile cases.

Hill said the Irish American Winter Hill Gang leader Whitey Bulger sent the stolen artwork to the Irish Republican Army (IRA), a militant political group. Bulger likely believed he could trade the paintings for money or a favor, Hill said. Hill theorized that the paintings got to Ireland between 1990 and 1995. Around 2005, Hill reported that he was in "delicate negotiations" that could lead him to the artwork.[4] Those negotiations did not come to fruition.

Hill's theory differs from other reports. Stephen Flemmi was once a confidant of Bulger's. Flemmi later testified against the Irish gang leader during an unrelated 2013 trial in which Bulger was accused of murder. When asked by US attorney Michael

THE IRA

Some people have theorized that the Gardner Museum heist was committed by the Irish Republican Army (IRA). In this scenario, the IRA directly hired local Boston criminals to carry out the robbery. The artwork was then transferred to the IRA to help finance its operations in Europe.

According to *Boston Globe* journalist and author Kevin Cullen, the IRA was stealing art in Europe at that time. It was taking artwork from Irish mansions and then fencing it elsewhere in Europe. *Gizmodo* magazine reporter Kelsey Campbell-Dollaghan speculated that because the stolen Gardner Museum artwork had been done by European artists, except for the Chinese gu, it would hold more value in those countries.

James "Whitey" Bulger was a famous Boston mobster. He died in prison in 2018.

Sullivan if Bulger knew anything about the Gardner heist, Flemmi said that Bulger had not committed the heist but had asked Flemmi to figure out who did. Bulger had wanted a cut of the profits, Flemmi said. Bulger reportedly said, "No one pulls off a heist like that in my territory without paying me tribute."[5]

Former FBI agent John Connolly was a crooked cop who was on Bulger's payroll. He also said that Bulger wanted to know who had stolen the artwork. Supporting Flemmi's assertion, Connolly said Bulger wanted to "get his percentage, but he couldn't find anything out."[6]

RACKETEERING

Racketeering is getting something, usually money, through force or threat. It includes criminal activities such as extortion, loan-sharking, book-making (illegal gambling), kidnapping, truck hijacking, arson, and gun and drug trafficking. Organized crime members often commit these kinds of crimes. Investigators suspected that some of the missing Gardner Museum items may have been involved in the fencing racket. Fencing is when a person buys stolen items very cheaply and then sells them for a profit to an unsuspecting buyer. However, there are no publicized reports of attempts to fence the Gardner Museum artwork.

In order to combat racketeering, the US Congress passed the Racketeer Influenced and Corrupt Organizations Act (RICO) in 1970. The RICO Act was at first successfully used to attack organized crime. Since then, the act has been used by prosecutors to bring charges against corporations, unions, and sports organizations as well.

Bulger's relationship with Connolly was tied to the mob boss's work as an FBI informant. Bulger, a leading member of an Irish gang, had been offered protection because he was feeding information to the FBI about Italian crime families in Boston. However, Bulger was also under investigation by the FBI during this time. Connolly warned Bulger about FBI wiretaps that had been placed on him and also tipped him off about his impending arrest for racketeering. Bulger fled the city and remained on the run for 16 years. As a result of his criminal relationship with Bulger, Connolly was arrested and served a ten-year prison sentence for his crimes.

When the news of Bulger's FBI connection came to light in 1998, eight years after the Gardner Museum heist, it tainted many people's view of the FBI's ability to find the notorious art thieves. Anne Hawley, the Gardner Museum director at that time, said that she believed the FBI investigation of the heist "was possibly corrupted and compromised from the start."[7] Hawley, suspicious of the FBI, publicly encouraged anyone with information about the heist to contact her directly instead of contacting the FBI.

Anne Hawley, *left*, former Gardner Museum director, speaks at a press conference shortly after the heist.

CHAPTER FIVE

OTHER SUSPECTS

The statute of limitations for being criminally charged under Massachusetts law in connection with stealing the Gardner Museum art expired in 1995. After that, a small number of known criminals publicly claimed they were responsible for the initial planning of the heist. Investigators also researched the possibility of the heist being committed by people who were not known criminals, such as one of the museum's security guards. While these discussions led to some new leads, those leads still did not result in a conclusion to the case.

The Planners

Louis Royce was one known criminal who claimed credit for planning the Gardner heist. Another was career thief Myles J. Connor Jr. Although Connor was in prison at the time

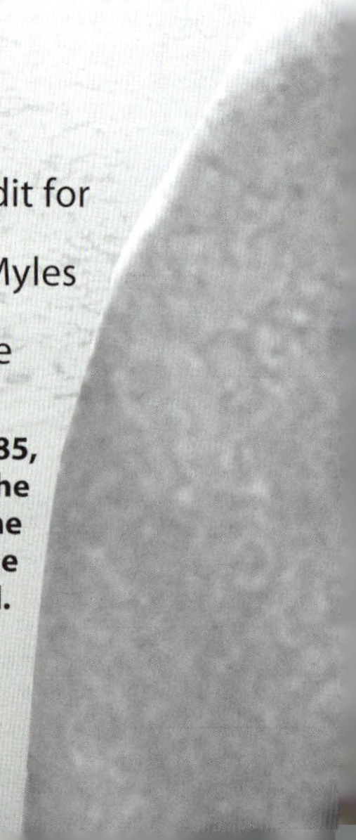

Myles J. Connor Jr., pictured in 1985, was one of several suspects in the Gardner Museum case, despite the fact that he was in prison when the heist occurred.

of the heist, he said the robbery happened as he had planned it in the 1980s. Connor had previously stolen a Rembrandt from the Museum of Fine Arts, Boston, in 1975. He traded that painting to authorities in order to get time off from prison. Regardless of who planned the robbery, one thing was clear: The security precautions at the museum were not very good and were well-known to the Boston criminal community.

STATUTE OF LIMITATIONS

A statute of limitations is a law that prohibits prosecutors from charging a person with a crime that was committed more than a certain number of years ago. The Massachusetts statute of limitations on art theft at the time of the Gardner Museum heist was five years.[1] This means that after 1995, the thieves were essentially free from the danger of going to jail under the applicable state law. However, the Gardner case moved the US Congress to make art theft from a museum or possessing the stolen art a federal felony in 1994. With that change, a person could be prosecuted for possessing stolen property (the art) seemingly forever.[2]

The Security Guard

In the aftermath of the heist, authorities quickly suspected Richard Abath. He was the security guard who had let the fake policemen into the museum. One of the reasons Abath was a suspect was that he was the only person whose motions were detected in the Blue Room from which the Manet painting was taken. Additionally, the museum's security sensors revealed that a day before the heist, Abath had opened the same door to the museum that he later opened for the disguised thieves on the night of the robbery. A security video released by the FBI in 2015 also showed Abath opening the door and speaking with someone on the night before the robbery. The police wondered whether this incident had been a practice run for the heist the next night. When presented with the video evidence in 2015, Abath said he couldn't remember the incident.

As of 2015, Abath was living in a town in Connecticut. From the looks of his low-key life, Abath did not appear to be benefiting from any possible heist proceeds. To this day, Abath denies any involvement in the heist.

Ever since the 1990 heist, frames have sat empty at the Gardner Museum in place of the stolen art.

The Con Man

Another possible suspect was Brian McDevitt. He was considered a con man; people who had met him described a charming, well-spoken, and believable person. Over his lifetime, he pretended to be a member of the well-known and socially powerful Vanderbilt family and also a screenwriter in Hollywood, California. While living in New York in the 1980s, McDevitt had attempted to rob the Hyde Collection in Glens Falls, New York. The plan was similar to the Gardner Museum heist. McDevitt and an accomplice hijacked a courier van and took the uniforms of the van's occupants. They

TESTING THE WATERS

The Gardner Museum robbery appeared to be carried out by professional criminals. They may even have conducted a test run to see how they might get into the building without breaking in. Several weeks before the actual robbery, a museum security guard saw on his video monitor a young man being beaten up by other men. The apparent victim banged on the museum door and cried for help. Instead of letting him in, the guard called the police. Before the police could arrive, both the victim and his assailants jumped into a car and took off. In hindsight, security officials believed the brawl was a scheme to test the museum's security.

Louis Royce and an associate, Richard Devlin, also appeared to have carried out an impromptu run at the museum shortly before the actual heist. Royce told *Boston Globe* reporter Stephen Kurkjian that while in the museum neighborhood one night, he and Devlin saw a bucket-lift truck at a construction site. They took the truck and raised the bucket to a second-story window. They could see that it was securely locked, so they abandoned the attempt to get in.

were headed to the Hyde when they got stuck in traffic and couldn't get to the gallery before it closed for the day. Just as in the Gardner heist, McDevitt was going to use handcuffs and duct tape to bind the security guards, as well as cutting tools to remove artwork from frames.

Law enforcement officials suspected McDevitt because of the similarities between the Hyde attempt and the successful Gardner heist. A second reason for the suspicions was that McDevitt's fingerprints were on the Gardner Museum's visitor log. Those fingerprints were among the first sent to the FBI crime lab after the robbery. At the time of the Gardner heist, McDevitt reportedly lived near the museum. He left Boston for California within days after the heist.

McDevitt's former girlfriend said he had told her in 1992 that an unnamed man had asked him to cut the Gardner pictures out of their frames for him. He also asked her to be his alibi for that night, but she refused. McDevitt died in 2004, denying any involvement in the Gardner heist to the end.

The Fake Painting

In August 1997, authorities thought they had a breakthrough in the investigation. A reporter for the *Boston Herald* newspaper, Tom Mashberg, wrote a story in which he revealed he had been shown the *Christ in the Storm on the Sea of Galilee* painting.

The story started months-long negotiations to get that painting and the rest of the Gardner heist pieces returned.

William Youngworth III, an antiques dealer in the Boston area, claimed to know where the artwork was hidden and supposedly showed the painting to Mashberg. But he wanted some concessions from the authorities before showing them all of the artwork. He asked for the $5 million reward. Youngworth also wanted immunity from prosecution for the theft itself and dismissal of some state criminal charges he was facing. Additionally, Youngworth wanted his longtime friend Myles Connor Jr. released from prison. Connor was behind bars on federal drug charges.

The authorities wanted evidence that the artwork was real. Youngworth gave them a few paint fragments that were supposed to be from one of the stolen Rembrandt paintings.

AMATEUR ART THIEVES

The Gardner Museum robbers were not art experts. They didn't seem to know that cutting a painting from its frame could totally destroy the painting and any monetary value it might have. Removed from their frames, old paintings can bend, causing the paint to flake off.

The thieves did not research their targets either. Rembrandt supposedly signed one of the stolen paintings, and Isabella Gardner thought it was an original when she first bought it in 1900. However, several years before the heist, the painting was found to be a fake. A Harvard graduate student, Cynthia Schneider, discovered that Rembrandt's signature had been forged. The painting *Landscape with an Obelisk* had really been painted by one of Rembrandt's students, Govaert Flinck.

FBI analysis at the time indicated they were not from a Rembrandt, and the negotiations were halted. Another analysis of the paint fragments was done years later. The test results showed they were like the paint used by other seventeenth-century Dutch artists. One of those artists was Vermeer, the painter of the missing Gardner Museum painting *The Concert*.

Mashberg later said that he believed the painting Youngworth had shown him was a fake. This was not only because of the discredited paint chips but also because the seascape by Rembrandt had been covered with a protective coating. That coating would not have allowed it to be rolled up like the painting shown to Mashberg. Another in a long line of Gardner Museum heist leads and suspects proved to be a dead end.

CHAPTER SIX

THE INVESTIGATORS

Many people have investigated the Gardner Museum heist. They range from official law enforcement agencies such as the FBI, to the museum security directors, to independent investigators, to investigative reporters. Some of them have seemed tantalizingly close to solving the mystery. But as of early 2019, none of them had been successful in finding the perpetrators or in getting the artwork back.

The Boston Police

The Boston Police Department was the first law enforcement agency to arrive at the scene of the Gardner Museum heist. Ushered into the building by the museum's assistant security director, police officers fanned out to search the building. Within minutes, they found the frames and broken glass where

A Gardner Museum security guard stands outside the crime scene a couple of days after the heist. Authorities used police tape to close off the museum as they investigated it.

CROSS
BOSTON POLICE

the artwork had been stolen. At the same time, officers in the basement found the handcuffed security guards.

The Boston police officers secured the museum property and began their initial investigations. However, despite their early entry into the chaos of the robbery, their participation was short-lived. By midafternoon, the FBI had taken over complete control of the investigation. According to Thomas J. Foley, former head of the Massachusetts State Police, the FBI did not seem to want assistance from the local authorities.

The FBI

The FBI's Boston office took control of the case early on and has continued leading the investigation. Retired FBI agent Tom Cassano, who worked in the Boston office at the time of the heist, said that initially there were at least 15 FBI agents working on the case.

After years of investigating the heist, the FBI formed its Art Crime Team in 2004.[1] Special Agent Robert Wittman worked for the FBI for a total of 20 years and was the first agent in charge of the agency's Art Crime Team. As he ran the team from 2005 until 2008, Wittman helped recover more than $225 million in art and antiquities.[2] As part of the Art Crime Team, Wittman went undercover in 2006 and 2007 in France to follow a lead on the Gardner Museum paintings.

Robert Wittman retired from the FBI in 2008 after working for the agency for 20 years, specializing in art theft.

Wittman posed as a rich art collector who was interested in purchasing some of the missing Gardner Museum art. His contacts, connected to the Corsican Mob, said they could produce Vermeer's *The Concert* and one of the stolen Rembrandt paintings. Based upon his undercover work and wiretaps, Wittman believed these men really did have access to the pieces, but they were middlemen, not the original art thieves. In 2008, the deal fell apart when one of the middlemen tried to sell Wittman some paintings from a recent robbery of a museum in Nice, France. Wittman turned the lead over to another agent, who arrested the criminal. The lead for the Gardner Museum items faded out as that arrest revealed Wittman's true intent.

In 2013, FBI Special Agent Richard DesLauriers announced that the FBI knew who had committed the heist. He would not reveal who the criminals were, but it later became clear to the public that he was referring to Reissfelder and DiMuzio. DesLauriers also said the FBI was very confident that the art had been transported to Connecticut and Philadelphia, Pennsylvania. There, he said, it had been offered for sale. DesLauriers then said the FBI didn't know what had happened

FBI ART CRIME TEAM

The Gardner Museum heist was one of the motivating forces in the creation of the FBI Art Crime Team. What were once considered low-level crimes became high-value thefts as art prices increased dramatically in the late 1980s. The estimated $500 million value of the stolen Gardner Museum items helped change how these thefts were viewed by the FBI. The FBI created its Art Crime Team in 2004. Longtime FBI agent Robert Wittman was the team's first director. In the beginning, Wittman was the team's only full-time agent. Today, there are 16 FBI agents involved with the Art Crime Team.[3] The FBI also maintains a database of stolen art and other types of objects called the National Stolen Art File (NSAF). It has the FBI's Top Ten Art Crimes list, which includes the Gardner Museum heist.

to the art after its arrival in Philadelphia. He would not offer any other details, claiming it might endanger further ongoing investigations. He did repeat that, at the time, there was a $5 million reward offered in hopes of enticing someone to come forward with new information. However, the reward offer was unsuccessful.

In 2013, the FBI posted a video description of the Gardner Museum case on YouTube in an attempt to attract new leads.

The Insurance Adjuster

Harold Smith, an insurance adjuster, became obsessed with trying to find the Gardner Museum items. He was an expert on fine arts losses. When the Gardner heist was announced, Smith knew he wouldn't be called to investigate. The Gardner Museum was not insured. Despite that, Smith was intrigued. After years of hearing about investigators hitting dead ends, Smith decided to get involved himself. He used his art and law enforcement contacts to follow the case. Even into his seventies, Smith worked up to ten hours a day trying to figure out who had robbed the Gardner Museum. He traveled all over the world and spent hundreds of thousands of dollars of his own money to follow leads. When asked why, he said, "There are hundreds of thousands of people who would be deprived

INVESTIGATIVE REPORTERS

Fascinated by the mysteries surrounding the Gardner Museum heist, two members of the Boston press spent many years pursuing the story and the lost artwork. Stephen Kurkjian of the *Boston Globe* and Tom Mashberg of the *Boston Herald* each used their law enforcement and criminal contacts to gather information that others might not have been able to gather. Mashberg was the reporter who had been invited to view one of the Rembrandt paintings that turned out to be fake. Together with the Gardner Museum's director of security, Anthony Amore, he wrote a book detailing the motives and methods of the Gardner heist and art world thefts in general. Kurkjian wrote a book too, recounting efforts to find the long-missing Gardner Museum artwork.

of seeing that art. Losing that art is like losing our history, our culture. I want it back."[4] Smith died from cancer in 2005. He had continued working on the case, even as his health diminished. Like so many others, his search went unrewarded.

The Art Investigator

In June 2017, Arthur Brand, a Dutch private investigator, claimed he was only months away from retrieving the stolen Gardner Museum artwork. Brand had an excellent reputation for recovering high-value stolen artwork, so his promise rekindled hopes among people working and waiting to find the stolen Gardner Museum art.

Like some investigators, Brand claimed the paintings were in Ireland. He said former IRA insiders told him that there had been talk of the paintings "for years within the IRA."[5] Brand was not officially working with the FBI in his investigation. Yet, as he did not want to criticize the FBI, he publicly credited the agency for continually coming up with additional leads. He also said the efforts to find the artwork were not a competition and that everyone's main goal was the safe return of the art.

Despite widespread speculation that the artwork must have been destroyed in the decades since the heist, Brand said he had some leads that the pieces still existed. He also believed, like the FBI, that the original burglars were dead. He stated that it wasn't "about who did it anymore."[6] It was about getting the artwork back. However, Brand's claim that the return of the works was imminent turned out to be just another dead end, as he never could produce the stolen art.

THE RETURN OF STOLEN ART

Although the stolen Gardner Museum artwork has been missing for years, there have been similar cases in which valuable stolen art was eventually returned. In 2017, a black market intermediary turned a stolen painting over to the FBI.

The intermediary, an unnamed Maryland man, attempted to consign the 1911 painting by Marc Chagall, *Othello and Desdemona*, to a Washington, DC, gallery. The gallery owner had concerns about the painting's authenticity because it was not accompanied by the usual paperwork for such pieces. The gallery owner suggested the Maryland man call the police, which is how the FBI's Art Crime Team became involved.

A thief had taken the painting in 1988 from a Manhattan apartment. The thief met with the Maryland man to sell the piece. The Maryland man found a buyer but discovered he was not going to receive a cut from the proceeds. So, the Maryland man stashed the painting in his attic for almost 30 years until turning it over to the FBI. The picture was returned to the now-dead owners' estate. Since the statute of limitations had passed, neither the Maryland man nor the thief were charged with a crime or publicly named.

Anthony Amore, security director of the Gardner Museum, addresses reporters during a 2013 press conference at the FBI headquarters in Boston. Museum officials have continued to publicize the heist over the years in attempts to retrieve the stolen art.

The Security Director

In 2005, Anthony Amore was hired as the security director for the Gardner Museum. He had previously worked with the US Department of Homeland Security. As security director, Amore worked closely with the FBI's top agent on the Gardner Museum case, Geoffrey Kelly. The two followed leads and interviewed numerous suspects and associates of suspects. Amore also spoke with reporters, art experts, and people in general about the case.

Twenty-eight years after the heist and 13 years after being hired as the Gardner Museum's director, Amore said he believed he knew who had committed the crime. But, like the FBI, he wouldn't publicly say more than that. He remains more interested in whether the art can ever be found. Will someone involved in the heist come clean? Will someone stumble across the artwork in some hidden spot? After looking at more than 30,000 pieces of information related to the heist, he believes just one more small clue "could end this tomorrow."[7]

Despite the millions of dollars in reward money offered for the recovery of the stolen artwork, few plausible leads have surfaced over the years. Because of that, Amore thinks the artwork hasn't been moved around much. "People assume that because a quarter-century has passed, those things are long gone. . . . [But] whoever the paintings went to could still be in possession of all or some of them," Amore told *Boston* magazine in 2016. Stolen art is often returned a generation after the original crime. By that time, Amore said, "The scariest person involved in the crime has died or is not so scary anymore."[8] Although the artwork might be gone forever, Amore fervently believes, or hopes, that a final clue will lead to its recovery.

CHAPTER SEVEN

WHY DID THEY DO IT?

According to Wittman, cutting the Gardner Museum paintings from their wooden frames would damage or destroy them. In that condition, they would be worthless to the thieves. In addition, Wittman said the paintings stolen from the Gardner Museum would probably be worthless on the black market because the heist had made them famous as stolen items, and anyone in possession of them would be incriminated.[1] So, why take them? There are several reasons why art is stolen.

Quick Money

Many thieves may be motivated by hoping to make money selling stolen artwork on the black market. However, that

A visitor looks at the empty frame of the stolen Rembrandt, *Christ in the Storm on the Sea of Galilee.*

REMBRANDT

approach does not usually work out well for the thief. This is especially true of well-known artwork because, typically, those pieces are immediately listed on the international Art Loss Register when they are stolen.

Alice Farren-Bradley works for the Art Loss Register based in London, England. She says that if a person could sell a piece of art on the black market, the seller would likely only get between 5 and 10 percent of the art's true value. Potential buyers might love to have the piece in their collection, but they'd never be able to show it off. Private investigator Arthur Brand reported that some of the missing Gardner Museum artwork was offered on the black market by an unnamed Dutch criminal. Despite that report, the artwork remains missing.

THE ART LOSS REGISTER

The Art Loss Register (ALR) was founded in 1990 in the United Kingdom. The funding for it came from insurance companies and leaders in the art markets. ALR's website says it has the world's largest private database of stolen art. The register makes it possible for people to see if an artwork they want to buy is stolen. In addition to registering stolen artworks, the company also helps museums, individuals, and law enforcement organizations recover their lost or stolen articles. It does that for a fee.

The fee-based approach has been criticized. The finders' fees have been described as exorbitant. Amore, head of security at the Gardner Museum, gave an example in his book *The Art of the Con*. He told the story of a Massachusetts collector whose precious Cézanne painting had been stolen in 1978. Twenty years later, the painting was recovered, but the owner had to sell the painting to pay the $2.6 million recovery fee charged by the ALR.[2]

Thrill and Challenge

Some people like the thrill of getting something while putting themselves at risk. They like the adrenaline rush. In the 1990s, a group of scientists, including Peter B. Wood, interviewed some jailed adults. One of their subjects said, "It was using your intelligence and everything else, pitting your wits against the police and the locks. . . . It definitely gave me an uplift, a charge."[3]

In 2009, one of the suspects in the Gardner Museum heist, Myles Connor Jr., wrote a book. In it, he said that while committing a museum burglary, his senses were elevated. Though he was not officially pinned as the culprit in the Gardner Museum heist, Connor was involved in many burglaries. He said, "It's a sweet feeling, one I've never gotten tired of, not on my twentieth heist, nor my fiftieth, nor my hundredth."[4]

Collateral

Expensive artwork does not need to be sold for money to have value on the black market. It can be used as collateral—something that is given to ensure a loan is paid back. Illegal weapons and drug deals can be financed this way. A weapons dealer or drug dealer can give valuable stolen art to a supplier in exchange for their product (weapons or drugs). The supplier then holds the art until the dealer can pay money for the

There are a lot of different reasons behind why someone may steal valuable artwork. Many of those reasons involve money, even if it's a case in which the stolen art is not directly sold for cash.

product they took. If the dealer does not pay up, the supplier keeps the art.

In 1986, a heist of 18 artworks from Russborough House near Dublin, Ireland, took place. Martin Cahill, who was the head of an Irish organized crime group, committed the robbery. He used a Vermeer painting from the robbery as collateral on a loan. The money was used to buy wholesale drugs for sale on the streets of Ireland. From the same heist, he smuggled a Gabriel Metsu painting to Turkey, where it was exchanged for heroin.

Ransom

Another criminal motive is to ransom the artwork back to its owners. Some museum professionals warn that paying a ransom seems to encourage art thieves to continue their line of work. However, museums, galleries, and individual collectors often want to get their valuable artwork back at any cost. This is especially true when the criminals threaten to destroy the art. Some art establishments skirt the ransom label by calling the payment a reward for insider information. There may be a fine line between an actual thief and a person who claims to be innocent but also has insider information. This may have been the case when the Gardner Museum got an anonymous letter.

In April 1994, the Gardner Museum received a letter that offered museum officials hope of recovering the stolen art. The anonymous writer said the paintings were safe. He or she also said the museum would have to move quickly because a buyer from another country, who did not know the paintings were stolen, might purchase them and get legal ownership. The museum agreed to pay $2.6 million to have the artwork returned.

A second letter from what appeared to be the same writer voiced the concern that several law enforcement authorities were involved. The unknown person was afraid that those authorities might want to arrest him as the middleman in

PROBLEMS WITH RANSOMS

Some museum curators, such as Geoffrey Clarfield, who has worked at the National Museums of Kenya, argue against paying ransom for stolen works. He thinks that paying the ransom further encourages more art crimes. The payments can result in what are called flag and boost effects.

The flag effect happens after a ransom has been paid for stolen art. Other thieves who hear about this view it as a success and then target similar museums or galleries for ransom. In 1959, six paintings were stolen from the Art Gallery of Toronto (known today as the Art Gallery of Ontario). A ransom was paid. Shortly afterward, a spate of robberies happened across Canada. Similar museums and galleries with poor security were "flagged" by crooks. The thieves were encouraged by the chance that they could get ransom payments too.

Some organizations attempt to thwart the flag effect by keeping ransom payments secret. Simon Mackenzie, a professor of criminology at a university in Scotland, thinks the payments will still result in what's called the boost effect. The original criminal's interest in a specific target is boosted by being paid off. The criminal goes back to the same museum to steal again. An example of this is the 1975 heist of 28 paintings from the Galleria d'Arte Moderna in Milan, Italy. The ransom was paid in secret. Within a few months, the gallery was struck again, and many of the same paintings were taken.[6]

the deal. He wrote, "Right now, I need time to both think and start the process to ensure confidentiality of the exchange."[5] He also said that he would provide clues to the paintings' locations if he decided to stop communicating. At that point, no further communication was received from that person, and no clues were found.

Bargain with the Law

Criminals have used stolen art as a plea-bargaining tool to spend less time in jail. *Boston Globe* reporter Kurkjian followed the Gardner Museum heist for many years. His book, *Master Thieves*, is about his investigative efforts. Kurkjian said that no one was going to pay for the stolen Gardner Museum artwork. However, if the thieves or their bosses were caught for other crimes, they could trade the loot for little or no jail time. "They call it a get-out-of-jail-free card," he said.[7] Kurkjian wrote in his book that he believed one of the Gardner Museum heist suspects, Bobby Donati, had exactly that motive.

Bargaining with art seems to be rare in the United States. Kurkjian, who is American, doesn't think that trades for artwork happen much in the United States. However, prosecutors in Europe appear to be more willing to reduce jail sentences for criminals if

PLEA-BARGAIN SUCCESSES

Although plea bargaining with stolen artwork has not happened often in the United States, it does occur from time to time. In 1974, six stolen paintings worth $500,000 were returned in a secret rendezvous at a federal courthouse to secure a plea bargain. The paintings, from the collection of Joseph Hirshhorn in Connecticut, were returned in good condition with only minor chips to the frames. A person who was granted anonymity returned the paintings. He delivered the paintings wrapped in plastic bags.

James Pickerstein, an acting US attorney for Connecticut at the time, said the pictures were returned as part of a plea bargain with Robert Hagerman. The 30-year-old Hagerman was found guilty of state larceny charges. But a federal charge of interstate transportation of stolen property was dropped as part of his plea bargain.

they exchange valuable art items. Gangs in Spain, for example, use stolen art to reduce sentences for unrelated crimes such as drug possession and car theft.

Fascination

Some art thieves do it just because they love art. A French waiter, Stéphane Breitwieser, was obsessed with great art. For seven years, starting in 1994, he stole art pieces from many of Europe's museums. He didn't do it for the money. He did it because he loved the art.

Robbers can have a variety of motives. It is still unknown why people stole the Gardner Museum art.

It was estimated that the total value of Breitwieser's stolen collection was $1.9 billion at the time of his arrest in 2001.[8] Breitwieser cleaned up the works, placed some of them in new frames, and stored them in his mother's house in eastern France. He then would visit the room and simply enjoy his stolen collection. He never sold any of them.

It is estimated by the *Art Newspaper* that only 1.5 percent of all stolen art is recovered.[9]

Breitwieser was finally arrested in Switzerland for stealing an old bugle. When he heard his mother had destroyed some of his stolen paintings to hide his crimes, he attempted suicide. He spent two years in jail in Switzerland. Upon being returned to France, he was then convicted of theft and was sentenced to 26 months in prison.

Whether the Gardner Museum heist was done for the love of art is not known. There could be several motives based upon who actually took the art. As the investigation continues, the museum is also working to prevent another heist.

CHAPTER EIGHT

THE SEARCH CONTINUES

One of the best ways to increase the odds of recovering stolen art is to keep the stories of the robberies alive. Attempts at this have been ongoing since the Gardner Museum heist in 1990. Newspaper articles, rewards, books, and movies have all been used to keep the Gardner Museum heist in the public eye.

Along with the publicity, new techniques for processing evidence and providing electronic security have evolved. Those techniques could help solve the Gardner Museum heist. They could also help prevent such crimes in the future.

Stolen, a Movie and a Book

Rebecca Dreyfus made a documentary movie about Harold Smith's attempts to find the missing Gardner art. For three years, Dreyfus shadowed Smith. Smith's personal obsession

Years after the heist, visitors continue to enjoy the Gardner Museum.

with the crime was highlighted in the documentary, titled *Stolen*, in 2005. He was followed across two continents. His meetings with underworld criminals, a Scotland Yard investigator, and a seemingly knowledgeable informant were all recorded.

Smith was convinced that someone knew where the stolen art was located. He thought media coverage could help convince that someone to come forward. He was sure they could retrieve the art if that person became aware of the $5 million reward offered by the Gardner Museum at that time.

In 2018, the Isabella Stewart Gardner Museum published the book *Stolen*, after the documentary of the same title. Like its movie predecessor, the book was made to keep the

PAINTINGS BACK, SORT OF

A self-described "group of art-loving Bostonians" used augmented reality (AR) to do what the FBI couldn't. The technology start-up developed an AR app that allows Gardner Museum visitors to see the stolen pictures in their empty frames. To honor the anniversary of the heist in 2018, the company Cuseum released its *Hacking the Heist* AR app.

A user simply aims his or her smartphone camera at the empty frame in the museum, and the stolen painting appears in the frame as if it were still there. At the time of its release, the app only included two of the stolen Rembrandt paintings: *Christ in the Storm on the Sea of Galilee* and *A Lady and Gentleman in Black*. The app's creator, Brendan Ciecko, planned on adding the nine other stolen paintings at a later time. He also hoped the museum would share the app with visitors, saying, "There's a big opportunity to inspire Boston public school children and people interested in the arts and sciences."[1]

heist in the public eye until the artwork can be returned to its rightful place. The book reviews the timeline of the theft itself. It also includes many colorful pictures of the missing works. Photographs of the rooms where the robbery occurred are also included, and the book even offers a plea for the return of the art. The book provides the contact information for anyone with information about the missing pieces and assures that anonymity will be granted.

DNA Analysis

Almost 20 years after the heist, authorities wanted to resubmit evidence from the robbery scene for further DNA analysis. The hope was that this further analysis could produce new leads because of technological advances in this type of analysis. Although the specific evidence under consideration was not revealed publicly, Dr. Bruce Budowle, an expert familiar with the case, indicated it was probably the duct tape used to tie up the security guards.

Budowle, once an FBI scientist, said that new results might be found from any sweat that was left on the duct tape and the handcuffs. The potential new samples could help determine some of the physical attributes of the robbers, including their facial bone structure. Using computer modeling of DNA strands, scientists are working to develop 3-D pictures of faces using DNA samples. Although this technology is still in its

DNA technology has advanced in the years since the Gardner Museum heist.

infancy, law enforcement agencies are very interested in using this tool to identify suspects. In addition, Budowle said the FBI could use its DNA database to compare any DNA samples to the seven million people convicted of felonies over the previous 20 years. *Boston Globe* reporter Stephen Kurkjian wrote, "Gaining a worthwhile clue would provide a boon to investigators who have coped with dashed hopes and phony leads in pursuing the theft of 13 pieces of art."[2]

However, the duct tape and handcuffs that authorities wanted to retest had disappeared. The FBI was unable to find the missing objects after a thorough search of its evidence files. It was unknown whether the items had been thrown away or simply misfiled. If misfiled, the evidence might still exist somewhere. But as investigators have been unable to find the evidence, this theory has become another disappointing dead end in the Gardner Museum mystery.

Increasing the Reward

In May 2017, the reward for any information that would lead to the return of the stolen paintings and artifacts was raised from $5 million to $10 million for one year only. This was done to increase the chances of getting the artwork back quickly. Brand, the Dutch art investigator, still thought that some of his leads were getting closer to solving the mystery. But he said, "If it's not solved by the first of January [2018] it will become . . . less likely that it will ever be solved."[3] A museum spokeswoman said the museum would gladly write a check for correct information that helped solve the case.

The deadline for the increased reward, December 31, 2017, came and went. It was a big disappointment to the museum and law enforcement. They had thought the increased amount would bring in some useful leads.

The reward being offered for the safe return of the stolen Gardner Museum artwork was $10 million again in 2019. But even this may not be sufficient to entice someone who has the items to turn them in. That's because it is a crime to knowingly possess stolen property. However, the US Attorney's Office in Boston has said it might possibly give immunity from prosecution if the artwork is returned.

Amore, the security director for the Gardner Museum, indicated that people with knowledge of the whereabouts of the artwork could contact the museum directly. Amore said that because he is not a member of a law enforcement agency, he

REVISE THE REWARD?

Art-crime expert Paul Hendry, a former antiques swindler, thinks he knows how to entice the Gardner Museum heist perpetrators into returning the art. He said that current law enforcement tactics could get in the way of the art being found or returned. He cited the Gardner Museum case, saying that anytime someone offered to share information, they were "hounded and threatened and even jailed."[4]

Hendry's proposal suggested three changes to the Gardner artwork reward. The first was to list the reward for each individual item, since they might not still all be together in one place or with one person. The second suggestion was to get rid of the "good condition" requirement, since it was a subjective assessment.[5] The last of the suggestions was to give full immunity from prosecution regarding anything related to the Gardner heist, with no exceptions.

could ensure an informant would not be arrested or named. He also said the reward money could be delivered anonymously. Amore's offer of anonymity might be good for the return of the artwork, but it also might ensure that the true story of the heist remains a mystery forever.

The deadline for getting the Gardner Museum's doubled reward of $10 million was midnight on December 31, 2017. The last call offering a lead occurred two minutes before the deadline.[6]

Preventing the Next Big Heist

As in the 1990s, protecting art worth hundreds of millions of dollars is still a difficult and complicated job. It requires security measures designed to keep people from taking objects while also encouraging visitors to get within touching distance of those same objects. It involves a balance of security and access to the facility. Modern security efforts involve the use of updated electronic security systems.

There are several types of electronic sensors that are used to protect valuable artwork. Some sensors detect the slightest pressure or movement. Motion detectors can be adjusted to guard just a single item or entryway. They can also cover an entire room or area. Those sensors with a wider range are called saturation sensors because they saturate an entire area with

In addition to security upgrades, the Gardner Museum has made many other changes over the years. These include adding a new wing, designed by architect Renzo Piano, in 2012.

motion detection. Early models of those sensors were in use by the Gardner Museum at the time of the heist.

Although museums and galleries do not like to advertise their security precautions, the Gardner Museum has continued to update its systems. In 2006, the museum added an access

control system. The museum has also hired a full-time security technology manager to oversee all security efforts.

Many art museums have implemented radio frequency identification (RFID) devices. The simplest form of this technology is similar to a bar code but smarter. It is a passive tracking device. Just like at the grocery store, a reader on the way out would tell security officers that a particular item was being removed from the premises. However, once outside the building, the passive RFID device could not be tracked in real time.

Active RFID devices that have their own battery and antenna could be the answer. Stolen artwork, just like a cell phone, could be tracked in real time by law enforcement authorities. However, experts have said these active RFID tracking devices, which require protective housing and extra-long battery life, are not necessarily feasible to use on artwork. The technology must be further developed. Additionally, RFID active tags come at a high price—more than $100 per unit.[7] Purchasing such a device for each piece in the Gardner Museum would amount to approximately $1.6 million just for the devices themselves. The price of tracking software and portable readers would likely add much more to the cost.

According to Steve Layne, head of the International Foundation for Cultural Property Protection, museums should focus their attention within their buildings. He said the emphasis should be on "stopping anything from leaving the walls."[8] To that end, retired FBI agent Wittman thinks one of the goals modern museum security is moving toward is computer-based video systems, such as facial-recognition technology, which could be used to catch repeat art thieves.

FACIAL-RECOGNITION TECHNOLOGY

Modern facial-recognition technology could have helped solve the Gardner Museum robbery or even prevented it. The technology's use has been growing steadily for law enforcement agencies, including border security and airport security, throughout the world. Facial-recognition technology works by comparing a previous picture of a person with one that shows up on a security camera.

If the Gardner Museum had well-placed hidden cameras on the night of the heist, investigators may have been able to compare the images of the robbers with known robbers and organized crime members using the facial-recognition technology. The law enforcement organizations that worked on the Gardner Museum heist were all convinced that perpetrators were local organized crime members. Undoubtedly, these known criminals' mugshots would have been available to the police.

Facial-recognition technology rapidly compares photos of known criminals in law enforcement databases with security camera images of people in the museum.

Steven Keller is an expert in providing security for all types of buildings. According to Keller, the most important thing to do for museum security is to prevent hackers from overpowering electronic security equipment. Many organizations try to save money by putting all their electronics controls—including telephones, burglar alarms, and video cameras—on one big network connected to the internet. That's a big mistake, says Keller. Criminal hackers have demonstrated their ability to get past cybersecurity measures on many occasions. Anything connected to the internet is vulnerable. So rather than putting every computer-controlled item on one system, Keller recommends isolating the security system on its own network not connected to the outside world, thus cutting down on potential tampering.

Why Is It So Difficult?

Stolen art, like that taken from the Gardner Museum, is often hard to recover because it is so easy to identify. The artwork can't be sold to honest art collectors and galleries because it is so well-known and listed on stolen-art databases. The thieves would not want to display the artwork anywhere that it could be seen because someone could recognize it as stolen and report it to the authorities.

The most likely people who steal valuable art are either museum insiders, such as maintenance workers, or common thieves with no art expertise. Typically, those criminals don't know how to contact potential black-market buyers or are afraid to try returning or ransoming the art. So, the art just languishes in a hiding place for years. It likely deteriorates as a result of fluctuating temperatures and humidity, which cause paint and canvases to shrink, expand, and crack.

Another reason art cases are so hard to solve is that most law enforcement agencies don't have the capability to solve them. Criminologist A. J. G. Tijhuis stated that most local and national police departments don't have much interest in working on art theft. Those that do still typically do not devote a lot of resources to art theft. The FBI in the United States has only 16 agents on its art theft team, and they are spread throughout the country.[9] In the case of the Gardner Museum heist, the FBI's Art Crime Team was not formed until years after the actual robbery.

The Gardner Museum had motion detectors that tracked the robbers' every movement, except for the entry to the Blue Room.

Another challenge is that local, state, and national law enforcement agencies do not always communicate and cooperate fully with each other. This appears to be the case with the Gardner robbery. A former head of the Massachusetts State Police, Thomas J. Foley, said the FBI was not willing to share the "glory" with state and local law enforcement agencies. He went on to say that the FBI might have benefited if they had used local expertise and contacts. "I think we could have helped, but no one ever asked for it," he said.[10]

How to Get It Back

One way to recover stolen art is to publicize the theft. Theft victims can contact law enforcement agencies, both local and international, to do this. The Gardner Museum itself regularly brings renewed attention to the continuing mystery of the 1990 heist. The victims can also post the thefts to a stolen-art

In addition to the empty frames, there are other reminders of the stolen art in the Gardner Museum. Security Director Anthony Amore keeps prints of the artworks hanging on the walls of his office.

database. This helps notify potential purchasers that the art they are attempting to buy is stolen. One of the drawbacks of this approach is that it may force the artwork underground, with thieves hiding it so it won't be found. The thieves might also just decide to destroy the artwork so that no one can link the evidence to them.

A final idea on how to get perpetrators to return stolen art was put forth by investigative reporter Kurkjian. He believed it would take more than money to get the family or friends of the now-dead thieves to return the artwork. Kurkjian suggested that public figures should make a heartfelt plea for the return of the stolen masterpieces that focused on redemption for the thieves rather than focusing on the crime. According to Kurkjian, this appeal to the thieves would be to "get those paintings back on the wall so your grandchildren and mine can see these paintings."[11]

The Isabella Stewart Gardner Museum heist was described as a crime against humanity. It robbed people everywhere of the chance to interact with artistic glimpses into the past. The Gardner Museum will continue the search for the stolen items. The reward for information leading to the return of the missing artwork was permanently raised to $10 million in January 2018.[12] Hopefully, one day the empty frames on the walls of the museum will be filled again with their rightful works.

TIMELINE

1901

- The construction of the Isabella Stewart Gardner Museum is mostly completed, and Isabella Gardner moves into the fourth-floor apartments.

1903

- On January 1, the museum's grand opening happens after Gardner's collection of paintings, sculptures, rare books, furniture, and decorative arts are placed in the lower three floors of the museum.

1981

- The FBI warns the museum administrators of a possible heist.

1990

- On March 18, the Gardner Museum heist happens in the early morning hours. Boston police and the FBI begin their investigation.

1991

- Law enforcement agencies lose a major lead when three of the prime heist suspects die. Bobby Donati and Leonard DiMuzio are separately murdered. George Reissfelder dies of a cocaine overdose.

1997

- *Boston Herald* reporter Tom Mashberg views what is thought to be one of the stolen Gardner paintings, but it turns out to be fake.

2004

- The FBI creates its Art Crime Team.

2005

- Insurance investigator Harold Smith dies of cancer after many years of unsuccessfully following up on possible heist leads.
- The Gardner Museum hires Anthony Amore as security director.

2006

- FBI special agent Robert Wittman goes undercover in France following a possible Gardner Museum stolen art lead.

2010

- Career criminal Robert Gentile is suspected of receiving the stolen artwork. Interviews and searches result in no answers.

2013

- The FBI claims it has solved the mystery of who the museum thieves were but refuses to identify them and does not discover where the artwork is located.

2017

- The reward for information leading to the recovery of the stolen artwork is raised to $10 million.
- Dutch stolen-art investigator Arthur Brand claims he is only months away from finding the stolen art, but he is then unable to find the art.

ESSENTIAL FACTS

SIGNIFICANT EVENTS

- The Isabella Stewart Gardner Museum artwork heist was the largest in history. The stolen artwork, together, was valued at about $500 million.
- The FBI warned the museum's administration of organized crime members' plans to rob the museum, even describing how it would be done.
- Despite the warnings, the museum's board of directors failed to provide the funding for adequate security measures.
- Law enforcement investigations have failed to identify the actual perpetrators, their motives, or where the stolen items are located.
- As of early 2019, the case remains unsolved, despite pleas to return the items and a $10 million reward.

KEY PLAYERS

- Bobby Donati, Robert Gentile, George Reissfelder, and Leonard DiMuzio were some of the prime Gardner Museum heist suspects with ties to the Boston Mafia.
- Richard Abath was the security guard working on the night of the heist. Some people have suspected he was behind the art theft.
- FBI agent Arthur Clark warned the Gardner Museum administration of a potential heist almost nine years before it took place.
- Fundraising expert Caroline Standley suggested ways for the museum to raise money for improved security before the heist, but the museum's board of directors did not listen.
- Anthony Amore, the Isabella Stewart Gardner Museum head of security, continues to work with the FBI in the continuing investigation.

IMPACT ON SOCIETY

The Gardner Museum heist resulted in the loss of important artwork that is now not available for study and enjoyment by people throughout the world. The heist also highlighted the lack of security at many culturally important sites, museums, and galleries that is still a problem today. As the case of the 1990 heist has remained unsolved for many years, it has stirred questions about how art thefts are committed and why valuable stolen artwork is difficult to recover.

QUOTE

"There are hundreds of thousands of people who would be deprived of seeing that art. Losing that art is like losing our history, our culture. I want it back."

—Harold Smith, independent insurance investigator who heavily researched the Gardner Museum heist

GLOSSARY

anonymous
Not named or identified.

black market
A collection of buyers and sellers trading illegally.

boon
Something that is helpful or beneficial.

collateral
Something pledged as security for repayment of a loan. If the loan is not repaid, the lender keeps whatever was pledged as collateral.

Corsican
Related to Corsica, a French island in the Mediterranean Sea.

cybersecurity
The measures taken to protect a computer or computer system against unauthorized access or attack.

etching
A form of printmaking that involves drawing on or lightly carving into a metal plate.

finial
An ornament at the top, end, or corner of an object.

Impressionism
A style of painting that originated in France in the 1870s characterized by dabs or strokes of unmixed colors showing a natural scene.

loot
Stolen money or valuables.

Mafia
An Italian American organized crime group.

monetary
Having to do with money.

motive
The reason for doing something.

perpetrator
Someone who is responsible for an act.

prophetic
Accurately describing or predicting what will happen in the future.

protocol
A set of routine behaviors, practices, or rules.

ransom
Money paid or demanded for the return of something stolen.

saturate
To completely fill or cover something.

sting
An undercover law enforcement operation that, if successful, results in an arrest or citation for illegal activity.

warrant
A document allowing law enforcement to carry out an arrest, a search, or an information-gathering operation.

ADDITIONAL RESOURCES

SELECTED BIBLIOGRAPHY

Amore, Anthony. "Gardner Museum Theft: An Active and Ongoing Investigation." *Isabella Stewart Gardner Museum*, n.d., gardnermuseum.org. Accessed 28 June 2019.

Böser, Ulrich. *The Gardner Heist*. HarperCollins, 2009.

Eveleth, Rose. "The Elusiveness of Stolen Art." *Atlantic*, 29 Aug. 2014, theatlantic.com. Accessed 12 Feb. 2019.

Kurkjian, Stephen. *Master Thieves: The Boston Gangsters Who Pulled Off the World's Greatest Art Heist*. Public Affairs, 2015.

Schwartz, Lloyd. "Here Are the 13 Artworks Stolen the Night of the Gardner Museum Heist." *WBUR*, 20 Aug. 2018, wbur.org. Accessed 15 Feb. 2019.

FURTHER READINGS

Harris, Duchess, and Rebecca Rowell. *The History of Criminal Law*. Abdo, 2019.

Hess, Kären Matison, Christine Hess Orthmann, and Henry Lim Cho. *Criminal Investigation*. Cenage Learning, 2017.

Perdew, Laura. *A History of Art*. Abdo, 2015.

ONLINE RESOURCES

Booklinks
NONFICTION NETWORK
FREE! ONLINE NONFICTION RESOURCES

To learn more about the Gardner Museum heist, please visit **abdobooklinks.com** or scan this QR code. These links are routinely monitored and updated to provide the most current information available.

MORE INFORMATION

For more information on this subject, contact or visit the following organizations:

THE FBI ART CRIME TEAM

935 Pennsylvania Ave. NW
Washington, DC 20535
202-324-3000
fbi.gov/investigate/violent-crime/art-theft

The FBI's Art Crime Team develops a Top Ten Art Crimes list, maintains an international database of stolen art, and conducts investigations.

THE ISABELLA STEWART GARDNER MUSEUM

25 Evans Way
Boston, MA 02115
617-566-1401
gardnermuseum.org

This museum was the site of the biggest art heist in history.

SOURCE NOTES

CHAPTER 1. THE BIGGEST ART THEFT

1. Kelly Horan and Jack Rodoclio. "81 Minutes." *WBUR*, 16 Sept. 2018, wbur.org. Accessed 30 July 2019.

2. Ulrich Boser. *The Gardner Heist: The True Story of the World's Largest Unsolved Art Theft.* HarperCollins, 2009. 12.

3. Boser, *The Gardner Heist,* 13.

4. Angie Kordic. "Legendary Art Theft Cases We Cannot Forget." *Widewalls*, 7 Dec. 2016, widewalls.ch. Accessed 13 Feb. 2019.

5. Allison McNearney. "Most Wanted: Vermeer's 'The Concert,' the World's Most Expensive Missing Work of Art." *Daily Beast*, 17 Nov. 2017, thedailybeast.com. Accessed 15 Feb. 2019.

6. Stephen Kurkjian. *Master Thieves: The Boston Gangsters Who Pulled Off the World's Greatest Art Heist.* Public Affairs, 2015. 51.

7. "10 Famous Art Heists." *History*, 22 Aug. 2011, history.com. Accessed 30 July 2019.

8. Patrice Shields. "FBI Legend Robert Wittman Exposes the World of High Stakes Art Thieves." *Naples Daily News*, 1 Feb. 2012, naplesdailynews.com. Accessed 30 July 2019.

9. "Art Crimes Investigator, Then and Now Retired FBI Agent Robert K Wittman." *Antiques and the Arts Weekly*, 5 May 2009, antiquesandthearts.com. Accessed 12 Mar. 2019.

CHAPTER 2. THE STOLEN ART

1. Lloyd Schwartz. "Here Are the 13 Artworks Stolen the Night of the Gardner Museum Heist." *WBUR*, 20 Aug. 2018, wbur.org. Accessed 15 Feb. 2019.

2. Matt Rocheleau. "In Today's Market, Could the Stolen Gardner Art Be Worth $1 Billion?" *Boston Globe*, 27 Nov. 2018, bostonglobe.com. Accessed 30 July 2019.

3. Lloyd Schwartz. "'Christ in the Storm on the Sea of Galilee,' by Rembrandt Van Rijn." *WBUR*, 15 Sept. 2018, wbur.org. Accessed May 26, 2019.

4. Rocheleau, "In Today's Market, Could the Stolen Gardner Art Be Worth $1 Billion?"

5. Rocheleau, "In Today's Market, Could the Stolen Gardner Art Be Worth $1 Billion?"

6. Rocheleau, "In Today's Market, Could the Stolen Gardner Art Be Worth $1 Billion?"

7. Rocheleau, "In Today's Market, Could the Stolen Gardner Art Be Worth $1 Billion?"

8. Rocheleau, "In Today's Market, Could the Stolen Gardner Art Be Worth $1 Billion?"

9. Rocheleau, "In Today's Market, Could the Stolen Gardner Art Be Worth $1 Billion?"

10. Rocheleau, "In Today's Market, Could the Stolen Gardner Art Be Worth $1 Billion?"

11. Katherine Q. Seelye. "Clock Is Ticking on $10 Million Reward in Gardner Art Heist." *New York Times*, 26 Dec. 2017, nytimes.com. Accessed 6 Feb. 2019.

12. Rocheleau, "In Today's Market, Could the Stolen Gardner Art Be Worth $1 Billion?"

13. Rocheleau, "In Today's Market, Could the Stolen Gardner Art Be Worth $1 Billion?"

14. Rocheleau, "In Today's Market, Could the Stolen Gardner Art Be Worth $1 Billion?"

15. "Collection." *Gardner Museum*, n.d., gardnermuseum.com. Accessed 19 Mar. 2019."

16. Stephen Kurkjian. *Master Thieves: The Boston Gangsters Who Pulled Off the World's Greatest Art Heist.* Public Affairs, 2015. 53.

17. Kathleen Allen. "Recovered de Kooning Painting to Be Restored by Getty Experts." *Arizona Daily Star*, 16 Mar. 2019, tucson.com. Accessed 30 July 2019.

CHAPTER 3. AN EARLY WARNING

1. Stephen Kurkjian. *Master Thieves: The Boston Gangsters Who Pulled Off the World's Greatest Art Heist.* Public Affairs, 2015. 24.

2. "Collection." *Gardner Museum*, n.d., gardnermuseum.com. Accessed 19 Mar. 2019.

3. Kurkjian, *Master Thieves*, 37.

4. Fox Butterfield. "Boston Museum Says It Was Uninsured for Theft." *New York Times*, 20 Mar. 1990, nytimes.com. Accessed 10 Mar. 2019.

CHAPTER 4. ORGANIZED CRIME IN BOSTON

1. Noah Charney. "What's the Motive behind Most Art Thefts? These Mafia Heists Provide Clues." *Observer*, 9 July 2018, observer.com. Accessed 3 Mar. 2019.

2. Erick Trickey. "The Gardner Museum Heist: Who's Got the Art?" *Boston Magazine*, 13 Mar. 2016, bostonmagazine.com. Accessed 11 Mar. 2019.

3. Robert M. Poole. "Ripped from the Walls (and the Headlines)." *Smithsonian Magazine*, July 2005, smithsonianmag.com. Accessed 18 Feb. 2019.

4. Poole, "Ripped from the Walls (and the Headlines)."

5. Stephen Kurkjian, *Master Thieves: The Boston Gangsters Who Pulled Off the World's Greatest Art Heist.* Public Affairs, 2015. 209.

6. Kurkjian, *Master Thieves*, 209.

7. Poole, "Ripped from the Walls (and the Headlines)."

CHAPTER 5. OTHER SUSPECTS

1. Justin Peters. "The FBI Knows Who Stole $500 Million Worth of Art from a Boston Museum. but the Culprits Probably Aren't Going to Jail." *Slate*, 19 Mar. 2013, slate.com. Accessed 19 Feb. 2019.

2. Jennifer Anglim Kreder and Joseph Huber. "Anticipating Prosecution of the Gardner Heist." *Canadian Criminal Law Review*, 5 Sept. 2013, ssrn.com. Accessed 22 May 2019.

CHAPTER 6. THE INVESTIGATORS

1. "Art Theft." *Federal Bureau of Investigation*, n.d., fbi.gov. Accessed 30 July 2019.

2. "Art Crimes Investigator, Then and Now Retired FBI Agent Robert K Wittman." *Antiques and the Arts Weekly*, 5 May 2009, antiquesandthearts.com. Accessed 12 Mar. 2019.

3. "Art Theft."

4. Ulrich Boser. *The Gardner Heist: The True Story of the World's Largest Unsolved Art Theft.* HarperCollins, 2009. 36.

5. "New Twist in Unsolved Gardner Museum Art Heist." *CBS News*, 21 June 2017, cbsnews.com. Accessed 3 Mar. 2019.

6. Sarah Cascone. "Vigilante Art Hunter Thinks He Can Recover the Stolen Gardner Museum Paintings within Months." *Artnet News*, 20 June 2017, artnet.com. Accessed 30 July 2019.

7. Erick Trickey. "The Gardner Museum Heist: Who's Got the Art?" *Boston Magazine*, 13 Mar. 2016, bostonmagazine.com. Accessed 11 Mar. 2019.

8. Trickey, "The Gardner Museum Heist: Who's Got The Art?"

SOURCE NOTES CONTINUED

CHAPTER 7. WHY DID THEY DO IT?

1. Stephanie Pappas. "Biggest Art Heist Ever: Will Released Tape Bring Paintings Back?" *Live Science*, 11 Aug. 2015, livescience.com. Accessed 27 May 2019.

2. Eileen Kinsella. "The Art Loss Register Is Entangled in Three Major International Art Disputes." *Artnet News*, 5 June 2015, artnet.com. Accessed 14 Mar. 2019.

3. "The Thief." *Criminal Justice School Info*, n.d., criminaljusticeschoolinfo.com. Accessed 30 July 2019.

4. Myles J. Connor and Jenny Siler. *The Art of the Heist: Confessions of a Master Thief.* HarperCollins, 2009. 1.

5. Pappas, "Biggest Art Heist Ever."

6. "Ransoms and Stolen Art." *Museum Security Network,* 28 Feb. 2009, toncremers.nl. Accessed 30 July 2019.

7. Pappas, "Biggest Art Heist Ever."

8. Robert M. Poole. "Ripped from the Walls (and the Headlines)." *Smithsonian Magazine*, July 2005, smithsonianmag.com. Accessed 18 Feb. 2019.

9. Rose Eveleth. "The Elusiveness of Stolen Art." *Atlantic*. 29 Aug. 2014, theatlantic.com. Accessed 12 Feb. 2019.

CHAPTER 8. THE SEARCH CONTINUES

1. "Hacking the Heist." *Hacking the Heist*, n.d., hackingtheheist.com. Accessed 19 Feb. 2019.

2. Stephen Kurkjian. "DNA Clues Hunted in '90 Art Theft." *Boston Globe*, 4 Mar. 2010, boston.com. Accessed 13 Feb. 2019.

3. Associated Press. "Boston Museum Offering $10M Reward for Help Solving Biggest Art Heist in U.S. History." *New York Daily News*, 26 Dec. 2017, nydailynews.com. Accessed 27 May 2019.

4. Eileen Kinsella. "Former Swindler 'Turbo Paul' Hendry Tells All about Art Theft." *Artnet News*, 25 Aug. 2014, artnet.com. Accessed 17 Mar. 2019.

5. Crawlspace Media. "Let's Bring Home the Stolen Isabella Stewart Gardner Museum Art: A New Approach." *Change.org*, 2018, change.org. Accessed 17 Mar. 2019.

6. Eileen Kinsella. "Got Intel on the World's Most Famous Art Heist? The Gardner Museum Just Extended Its $10 Million Reward for Missing Paintings." *Artnet News*, 11 Jan. 2018, artnet.com. Accessed 5 May 2019.

7. "How Much Does an RFID Tag Cost Today?" *RFID Journal*, n.d., rfidjournal.com. Accessed 10 Mar. 2019.

8. Rose Eveleth. "The Elusiveness of Stolen Art." *Atlantic*. 29 Aug. 2014, theatlantic.com. Accessed 12 Feb. 2019.

9. "Art Theft." *Federal Bureau of Investigation*, n.d., fbi.gov. Accessed 30 July 2019.

10. Justin Peters. "Why Is Stolen Art So Hard to Find?" *Slate*, 14 Aug. 2015, slate.com. Accessed 10 Mar. 2019.

11. Stephanie Pappas. "Biggest Art Heist Ever: Will Released Tape Bring Paintings Back?" *Live Science*, 11 Aug. 2015, livescience.com. Accessed 27 May 2019.

12. Anthony Amore. "Gardner Museum Theft: An Active and Ongoing Investigation." *Gardner Museum*, n.d., gardnermuseum.com. Accessed 13 Mar. 2019.

INDEX

ABOUT THE AUTHOR

Michael Regan worked as a community college and university career counselor before turning his attention to research and writing. He is especially interested in topics related to technology and current events. In his spare time, he enjoys watercolor painting, hiking, tai chi, and reading. He lives in southern Arizona with his spouse and two cats.